Zig Has Big Feet

by Karen Muldrow

Zig had big feet.
He felt shy to go out.
He'd look out his window
and try not to pout.

He wanted to dance
like his neighbor, you see.
But she had small feet
and danced better than he.

His neighbor could dance.
She could twirl. She could spin.

Zig heard she once danced on the head of a pin!

Did she just dance alone?
No! She danced with her pals.
She danced with the guys and
she danced with the gals.

She danced with her friends
and with those she just met.
She danced with her family
and her family's pets.

Well, Zig wanted to dance
but was scared to begin.
And because Ziggy worried
he didn't join in.

Do you know why he worried?
He thought she might say
that his feet were too big
and would get in the way.

Yes, Zig's feet were quite big.
They were not like his mother's.
They were not like his dad's,
or his sister's or brother's.

His feet made him stand out
whenever he stood.
So, he tried hard to hide them
whenever he could.

Zig stood behind bushes,
and babies and rocks.
He hid his feet inside
a very large box.

So, what happened next?
Well, some people say
that the neighbor asked Ziggy
"Will you dance today?"

"But my feet are so huge!"
Ziggy said with despair.
"If I raise my foot high
it might catch in your hair!"

"Well, that would be something," the neighbor replied,
"You could swing me right up like a kite in the sky!"

"But my feet are so long!"
Ziggy answered with dread.
"If I started to dance
I might trip you instead!"

"What a thought," said the neighbor
"I just might decide
to hop onto your foot.
You could give me a ride!"

"And if," Ziggy asked,
"people think that I'm strange?"
"Well, it's true," said the neighbor,
"We're not all the same."

Some people are short.
Some people are tall.
And some of my friends
are not people at all.

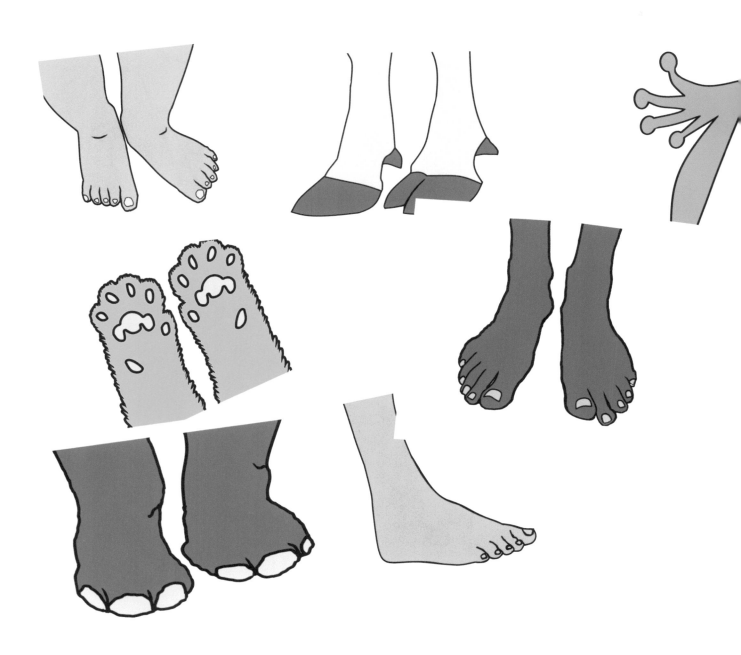

And maybe your feet
are not odd or bizarre.

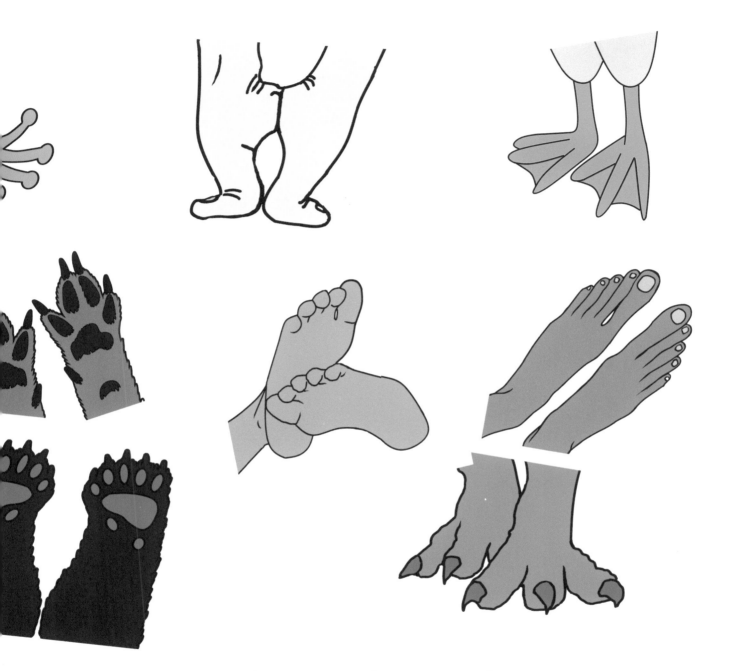

Maybe your feet are just
how some feet are.

If you stand on your toes,
if you stomp with your heels,
If you twirl all around,
you might suddenly feel

happy and joyful
and giddy and grinning.
We'll all be delighted
if you start join-in-ing.

Zig found it was true.
He could dance with big feet!
He could leap! He could spin!
He could follow the beat!

And when people watched,
he was glad, in the end,

to invite them to dance
and become a new friend.